T0153131

A Measure's Hush

A Measure's Hush

poems by

Anne Coray

Book design by Mark E. Cull
Book layout by Kathrine Davidson

Library of Congress Data
Coray, Anne.
    A measure's hush : poems / by Anne Coray.—1st ed.
       p. cm.
    ISBN 978-1-59709-463-4 (alk. paper)
    I. Title.
    PS3603.O7315M43 2011
    811'.6—dc22

                              2010045107

Boreal Books is an imprint of Red Hen Press
www.borealbooks.org
First Edition

Acknowledgments

Grateful acknowledgment is made to the editors of the following magazines in which these poems first appeared, some in slightly different form:

The Bitter Oleander: "Seven Couplets to Awakening"; *BigCityLit* (online): "Of the North"; *Cape Rock*: "December"; *Cirque*: "Painting, Intermediate," "Unpublished"; *Columbia*: "Vestiges"; *Commonweal*: "Credo," "Expectations of a Leaf," "Hold in the Hand Your Many Vows," "Print/Woodcut," "Statue Freestanding"; *ICE FLOE*: "Collage," "History of Wind"; *Many Mountains Moving*: "Abstraction," "Eskimo Mask, St. Michael"; *Midwest Quarterly*: "So It Is Written"; *Poem*: "The Artist Speaks of Gray"; *Poetry*: "The Egyptians Had It All Wrong"; *Poetry International*: "June Drought," "Terms"; *Potomac Review*: "Tlingit Shaman's Mask," "Tsimshian Sea Monster Mask"; *Rattapallax*: "*Sterna paradisaea*"; *Rattle*: "Call It Love," "Letter from a Brother"; *Redwood Coast Review*: "The Art of Being"; *River Oak Review*: "The Meantime," "Weights, Measures"; *Southern Poetry Review*: "Negative Space," "Painting, Beginning," "Watercolor"; *The Southern Review*: "Grass Studies," "Strand"; *Wisconsin Review*: "Early Sunday Morning"; *The Women's Review of Books*: "Away from the Day Shift's Bullhorn and Dazzle," "A Hand Half in Darkness."

"Seven Couplets to Awakening" was a finalist for the Frances Locke Memorial Award.

Several of these poems appeared in a limited edition chapbook, *Soon the Wind*, from Finishing Line Press.

Thanks to Peggy Shumaker, Ruth Holzer, and Mike Burwell for their careful reading of this manuscript and for their insightful editorial suggestions. And special thanks, as always, to Steve.

To Charles Wright, whom I have never met, but whose work and worldview were the spirit behind many of these poems.

Contents

I have sung, to deceive the evil-sounding clock of time,
   In twenty ways.
                    —Jean Cocteau, "Plain Song"

And the word, alive, but infinitely dead
When at last the light is made nocturnal wind.
                    —Yves Bonnefoy, "Quiet . . ."

Eternity
never was lost.

What we did not know

was how to translate it into days,
skies, landscapes,

into words for others,
 authentic gestures.
                    —Eugene Guillevic, "Eternity . . ."
                    translated by Denise Levertov

December

Everything loses itself in the ice,
in the ice that consumes the glitter,
taking it whole in its dry mouth.
Between here and eternity
I am jinxed.
Too many French poets
dying in the alleys of their voice,
throats sliced with a single cut.
But surely there is some message
still trying to crawl out:
a spore in the blood, in the worm.

I am not sure.

To the west, just visible on the horizon,
shreds of sky slip cleanly
behind the earth.
While our fingers
only lick these words,
like wind over bodies
that are laid out,
unbraceleted, not fully embalmed.

A half-scent, then,
holding us in this register,
almost at arm's length.
Afternoon, and the whole shore
stretched and tacked.

What skin, what animal,
lisping the silence?
Across the bay,
a charcoal of tree and rock.

Uncoloring

I want to go for days
with no music,
to sit on a tan shelf of earth.
No memories, no chartings

only an opening
to the white peel of birch,
the flesh of clean silence,
the sun's impassive light.

I would like a broom
with no voice
that carefully sweeps the wind

a cloth of still water
to brush the errant mote
from the crystal lens.

JUNE DROUGHT

No rain again, and the light like a scrub
hanging upside-down from heaven.
Even the trees cough dust.
There is little to imagine but a story read before,
the grit of something grave in the teeth.

On and on, summer keeps whittling the soul.
As if it is trying to tell us—what?
That ash makes a poor rattle.
That it scores the deepest crevices of our words
until the breath lies blank and every rib is christened
with a gray and restless fear.

O faith, so slow and difficult.
Like the creek now, all spittle and stone.
And the wildflowers—can they stay us?
Buried in their labyrinth of bloom . . .
Half-swirl, and the heart settles back,
roots still tunneling in a direction deeper than earth.

COLLAGE

The wind will edit him soon enough.
　　　　　　—Charles Wright

only flies and raindrops
yesterday the shadow of a hawk
the sky swims by
in a stream of wind

there is a woman trying to paste things up
the soulless color of mountains
the trees like a subtext in a will
here a thumbprint

and always the bold strokes saying
　　　　you cannot make meaning

in the lit window
she stands and stirs her coffee
these hours will be put down
as large canvasses of mauve

　　　　　　～

a life is too much, and not enough
she understands that

today she tries the particulars
but they are edged aside, obscured by wider images:
a birth, a residence, a death

then linen, gessoed and waiting
for another's loaded brush

and what else? the hornets
will bore on through the ages,
rust or drought trouble the native rose,

but the moon's white bead
necklacing the earth

is worth something
even to an unbeliever

EXPECTATIONS OF A LEAF

All winter it hung
from the twine of a branch,
as if waiting for more than the wind's hard mallet

to strike it down; tip curled up, it assumed
the shape of a bell, but made
no sound.

It could not fold; its edges failed
to create a dragon or ship.
The ground did not rise in greeting; the grasses,

bent to a shower of snow, stayed put.
And all those leaves, fallen already, kept hidden
their wings, mysteriously grown

when they'd given up, sky-jumped and glided
into the field, its soil loosely packed, composed
of eternally crumbling ancient skins.

SHRIFT

Transgressions again—
foil and mirror, envelope
of false charms.
I've brought them up
the long stair
to this little room.

Outside the late March wind
whistles on, a tune
neither woeful nor merry.
What does it care
for the sail's swagger,
the puffed, dihedral dress?

What ship anyway—
only invention's frail rigging.
Can I look out, past the frame
and glass to see
the lake's plain shimmer?
No, better to close the eyes.

Listen: come back to the lung,
its sure, light swell.
Already I can sense
how complete the hull
that cracks into a thousand shards
and spills its jewels.

Of the North

Brief, the Alaskan summer, but long the light
of early July, when one can sit up late
to sky-watch and wish only that wishes
attain the night's suspension.
Insects cluster and cruise, then join again,
their bodies a small galaxy
against a backdrop of indeterminate blue.

Whoever is here should be quiet now.
Whoever's thoughts have drawn up a chart
to the headwaters of the self's image
should set it down.
Look—what if we're going nowhere?
What if time is our most famous fabrication?
Up there, somewhere, all our longings

and desire for detachment from desire
spiral into a print that seeks no resolution.
Maybe the final lesson is to learn to spin
while stars, invisible, form the shape
of a great bear, and go on burning and dying
regardless of the season
or when on earth their shining will ever be seen.

Tlingit Shaman's Mask

(as healer)

inchoate flames
—flowers, pollen, roots—
hands, invisible, reach for the invisible

a cure of oxygen and copper
a totem of light
climb/return

for this beard the otter died
it knew
the human kingdom waits

in cedar and moss
you are lying
your breath the great canoe

we come, we come,
riding the sea waves,
your ancestors

through this smoke hole
that shadow
we are blowing

against the night sky,
a raven
against the moon,
a moth

(together we see them)

who is the woman with that face
that woman with those arms?

step into her,
            remember

rain beads fine
around your neck
beach rocks round
beneath your feet

again of the earth
little daughter
drink

Tsimshian Sea Monster Mask

(with six small figures carved as fins)

there must be a place
                where we are flying

        into the white gill of the sea
beyond the bottom, through soft

             claws, to the dead

        all our lives we have been wondering
those copper-plated eyes won't tell
                nor the mollusk teeth, leading

        our hands hold loosely, we are borne,
our bodies already absorbed

             no energies, no anger—sleep
though not as we remember it

        great worlds: rivers scarlet, fires green
             music composed of dusk, of light
        the clearest smoke circling

like breath
             and in the distance, moons, skies
        where nothing can condense—

Eskimo Mask, St. Michael

A single sound. The white shade of a drum.
One begins to notice things. The shape of a tear.
How even the wind has surfaces. The fans of the women
swaying like background light. Somewhere
a rock has fallen a long distance. Snow geese
sweep the sea . . .
                    Among the feathers, the stars,
through half-closed eyes, we know the short of it,
how easily the thong is drawn up—
those delicate tufts of fur, white blooms,
silencing the mouth.

LETTER FROM A BROTHER

It is the tailspin of autumn;
we know where this is going.
When I last wrote
I could still stand alone.
The funniest thing
is watching the leaves
which seem uncertain
where to land—
as if it mattered!
Mother frets
about the drip at my window
and can't fathom the delay
in the Grieg she ordered.
(Lyrische Stücke—
Jesus-Christus-Kirche recording.)
I was thinking the other day of hope,
how like blood it is
leaving for the first time the body,
how it believes in that new color
for a slick moment
before it begins to congeal . . .
Do you remember that dream I had
cold winter, no snow?
We were looking for a tree
—it must have been Xmas—
to either decorate or burn.
When I swung the axe
we discovered the tree was glass.
Back home, the wind had blown

your votive candles out.
I think I knew then
our bodies are a kind of crystal ash.

Write, if you get a chance.

Love,
Paul

CALL IT LOVE

Even while he lay, stern-browed and static
on the bed, rejecting death,
those of us still standing
in the hushed room
saw his arms become more shapely
and the dark hairs starting their undarkening
as moonlight flooded the window
and rode up his body until it touched
the tip of his chin.

Soon we knew she had come a long way
to meet him.
From a long night napless and cold.
Daringly her hips moved on him;
his toes took on her blue chill and curled.
Then the shadows in the hollows
of his face softened, and his breath slowed.

Soon the Wind

Now the window is no longer the window
you will pass through
like light
brushing the boughs and the leaves
from a room that held your body

       O psalm
       bell
       rising to the tenor of a star

In the half-moon
of your half-breath
furnishings settle your shapes
sky, impermanence
no longer arraigned

       Without alms
       without stones
       willingly in this hour

All asking done
soon the wind
will carry the scent of your bones
quietly
beyond

white bird in a white field

Elegy

Always the moon stuns in autumn.
It waxes now, shines on this turned earth.
Brother, your time was a cut plum. Your passions
were gone, though the thin words weigh:
you wanted to live.

Music and verse, nuggets of permanence,
brighten the charred bone chips and ash that I spilled.
Burial's never quite clean.
Come with me, down to the water. Night,
and the moon is a hot drum.
Rosehips are forming. A loon calls.
Something rises—it's Brahms.

WEIGHTS, MEASURES

There are rooms full of long thoughts,
and already I'm reducing them: full
of long thoughts, long
thoughts, then just
thoughts.

Paring down is one way;
to lay a hand on a table and ask
What if we lost this palm, these nails,
these cuticles, these fingers?
Would it make a difference in time—
in the ache for a line that is always out of reach
past sadness, bitterness?

Measuring began like this: birth, death.
Simple. Yet of course, hard; they are not opposites.
Then someone invented rood. Such a beautiful word.
It was made of wood.
Then stone. Granite or marble.
But does heart weigh heavier than slate?
Is ground equal to the breadth of reason?

I have no yard. Up the hill my brother's in ash.
About a song's walk, an aboriginal distance.
Which song? You ask. The shorter one—
shorter, that is, than the one that Omensetter sang.
It was his luck. He was
a wide and happy man.

O for such a sentence. It makes one want to go on,
to try a hand at words that can't be cubited
like *gift. Rabbit. Teddy bears and tights*:

a child in Switzerland just testing the register
of the French language. *Raisin . . . raisin . . . tomage.*
Unable to form the consonant blend *fr.*
Believing yet that word is food.
Not understanding it as portion,
the morsel on the dish,
the half-filled spoon.

Memorial

There's eternal emptiness in wind,
its open palm forever releasing
a strand of vapor, smoke, and dust.

This morning I shook the dust
from my rug and leaned into the window.
The glass caught briefly my vapor.

Smoke from the woodstove rose to the north
where dust purled and raveled in wind.
I opened my hand, let fall my rug,

imagined my body as vapor
released to a mountain ridge.
What would I catch? There would be things

other than dust and smoke: tufts
of fur, feathers, or pollen. A transport
more tangible than death.

Give thus your body as you would your breath,
that it may rise like smoke on a clear spring morning,
with only the vapor of mourning.

PASTEL

Somehow the days undraw themselves.
The white clouds erase the shapes
of things I knew, or thought I did.

When I think of you now, your face
is a face seen through water,
losing hour by hour its tone.

I want to bring back your cheekbones,
your sharp eyes. But they smudge and fade
and the face I sketch is not yours,

only the vague thought of it.
Do you know the Latin word for face?
Facies, meaning form, shape.

All through this long October
you resist my rendering.
Your body is snow and frost.

The clouds drift by.
The sun is strong.
I lift my hand to the wind, the light.

Watercolor

It's the next logical step. A thin, cardinal wash,
then just a blot to suggest a cloud.
The chance happening, where lake and mountain bleed and blur the margin.
But there's also the time you have to wait
to lay down something simple as *a line of dark and slender trees,*
and then that instant. Nothing uncommitted as the mind
saying no, try this: *the stark and slender trees.*
This palette is all earth tones: walnut, terra cotta, dun.
The grass stain on the bent knee. Perfectly transparent.

Painting, Beginning

You want to try some technique, like *grisaille*. But the teacher says no,
I don't teach that. You opt for a brush loaded with alizarin crimson
and the teacher laughs. So you too can blush. There's some red and
blue combo that makes him pause for a moment before he shrugs.
By then you're determined. You swear to give him your best Jackson
Pollock but you haven't the strength to lift the pail. You stare at a
well of white; it's not even the right tint. So with your ragged heart
you start to rub out every color you ever loved, including Prussian
blue, until the teacher finally nods. That's enough. You might want
to have a look at Titian. Particularly his use of flesh. Yes, you sob,
but in what proportion? The teacher snorts. In proportion to this,
of course. And he places in your hand a clod of earth.

Negative Space

The first thing, they say, is that you must use it. Even the background curtain becomes a shape. And between the ivory torso and the peach there is a place you wish to color cadmium, to match an *Early Sunday Morning* calm. You begin to see it as object, something you could transform into an instrument, or its part—that section just above the fret—if you look long or hard enough. But you'd rather not. You're hoping for nothing so reductive. So you move to a far corner of the canvas, load your brush, and for one fluid moment you have it: a broad and extravagant wash of sheer vermilion.

STATUE FREESTANDING

Hollows: the form within the form.
How is it that out of the frieze
the body is still dependent—
even in *contrapposto* appealing to the air?
I pledge to learn this inverse of expression,
to weigh each lifted arch against its death.
May we not fall,

but let the light
hold us a moment in its easy arms.
May we stay a little the grave weight
of fetishes and laurel.
May we not rise.

Early Sunday Morning

after Edward Hopper

So this is Sunday, wide and parallel,
hand-like curtains balanced in off-white hues.

Here is the intentional caress of order,
a rectangular awning of blue.

Did the painter choose?
Or did light guide his fingers

to these heights of green and orange,
to the doorways' deepened choir?

Believe what you will,
but ask what graceful brush

is governed by the man. Wonder
if the sun spread out this palette

and left each shade
drawn to its perfect proportion of silence.

THE ARTIST SPEAKS OF GRAY

he said believe in gray   it is our first diary
the most genuine color   the eggs of the greater yellowlegs
are often gray   as is glacial water   all our memories
whether cool or warm   there is the gray of seals,
whales, sharks   granite, flint   summers filled
with long hours of rain

gray is blessed   it is understood only by its soul
what is a pound, a pint of gray?   it exists in dreams
and infinity a cover with no edges   it smells
of musk   it belongs to eyes and ash and harmony
dry sticks and shadows   hunger and death

he said gray is my lover   she is a moth   a silver fox
not to be possessed   she knows one world
without horizons   a world of smoke and whispers

Red and Blue

It's the weekend, but the roses don't understand.
They are content in their redness. They face the wind.
All that is green contains some blue.
My heart's a little tree, it's bending.

My hand's a petal. I hold it up.
The wind is moist and cool.
Even my grief will be wrenched from me.
The world is cruel, I'm not yet old.

Red's a happiness like lending.
My hand is high, my heart is low.
It's the weekend, time is blue.
I bend and the wind keeps rending.

Painting, Intermediate

Atmospheric perspective.
Hills full of portals and stones.

Whatever you thought you understood is dissolving
in a wide, albescent sky.

And although the features of the woman
in the forefront are discernible enough,

her eyes remind you of distance—
the way they make their own pilgrimage

to a place the heart
cannot even begin to conceive.

And you wonder what there ever was to prove
in this landscape so godly indeterminate

as light and depth
and the unconstructed temples of the soul.

ABSTRACTION

A canvas of sky
I cannot bear to put a mark upon. The color
is already spoken, cerulean and still.
Nothing the wise need interpret. The paint
that hardened on the sable could have been anything:
apple, grape, or the blood of any fruit.
A line, a crucifixion. Picture, if you will,
just this: the testament of the yield of silence.

Print/Woodcut

What if the work doesn't save us
and we must set down the stencils,
brayer, and the ink: return
to wood not carved, to faces

featureless, where the eye relearns
its opposite—yes—just as words
must be written backward so that
they'll come out right, and the letters

—we remember now—are only glyphs,
stalks of wheat that once stood full
in a field until a minstrel wind
caught the tips and curved them down

in a form like *c*,
a bent of sound we'd heard
and heard but had no picture of,
that keening hung in rain and sun;

could this be our remaking—
one of one: the blade that is the word,
the pine before it's cut?

The Egyptians Had It All Wrong

All your life you must return to the moon.
To rill and light that have little to do with the sun.

To the scarabed wrist and the hawk
that tomb and tunnel the parched heart

you must say no. Though it will be difficult
to take up the lexicon that has crossed out:

star, monument, scent of spice and resin.
Laden so, you will never decipher

the pull of a line that refuses to be scrolled
or stamped by the pharaoh of some foreign country.

And you must abide the charms
that are always eyeing you from a secret cubicle,

that beg to be bundled and taken along.
But see, we aren't going.

This is not about aftermath or even anything
that blooms, exotically, like lotus.

I live North. I choose this home because it's what I know.
Of brick and scale I can say

there are other unfathomable things
that speak to both moment and beyond:

cold and wind and snow.
If anything remains, it will be nothing I create.

Like a scribed obelisk I can only hope
to crumble and spill back into a current

that moves and lifts so gently I scarcely feel it,
until I look up and still and again

enter the pool of that unframed face
assuring so quietly: *This. Only this.*

History of Wind

1.

the wind
wants
nothing

no blemish

it does not care
    to lift
        the Argo's sails

    or to be
a poor man's ghost

    its color
is too old
    to name

the wind is not even
an apostrophe

it connects nothing,
    claims
no spurious possession

2.

warm wind
cold wind
gentle, sad, and furious

sea and inland
traveler—still

the wind is without

belief

3.

Language, you have
fat hands,

hands that
grab and clutch,
hands that steal

when the wind
has picked you up
and you glide

on the pure throat
of pleasure,

you will let go

4.

Where The Wind Has Been

a dry bone   a sorrow
a field
            pillars of
broken memories   islands
lovely in the light,
golden and maroon

birches in winter
something held once

in the palm: a stone,
the smell of dead seeds,
a human mouth, empty . . .

5.

mathematics and half-eaten coins
the long bony finger beckons

what would it mean
to fall on the shoulders of trees
to find in the wind

the one long poem
erasing the day the hour
the minute the bucket the well

desire tightens
its cold tool—

at night power grows
more beautiful

and we forget for a while

the suction and the wheel
the river of sludge

forget the music we cannot hold

So Many Words Unspun

Last slivered light on the opposite shore
wound up by the consummate earth.
We come to this time knowing we have taken in nothing
but particles all day, and have not delivered speech.
All day, we believed the mouth
was something immense, a spindle.
Now there is not even prayer.
But it is enough to have this diaphragm to contend with:
ladder of bone and tissued flesh.

And it is good now to think moist thoughts,
to hold them to the count of a thousand stars.
Then there is only a tower of wind in the chest,
a sloped beat in the heart, and no imaginings.
Night's black silk will cover as it should
our cold desires: left curled in a bed of salt
they no longer suffer.
We have only to remember breath.

Small thing to lift each morning
from the mesh of sleep.
Small thing for which to listen.
But in the hard-lit noon,
surrounded by garbles and hooks,
can we return?
To find in the syllable one fine thread
and a quietude in the word
would be something numinous, and just.

Alphabet

A calm lake, rimas dissolutas,
rehearses the memory of its waves.

Bough and branch
accent the holographic sky.

Even rock, proud mummer,
articulates the drama of an ancient plosion.

How shall we learn this listening—
snow falling on snow,

distillate phoneme, white vowel,
mother tongue presuming no auricle?

We're all word-wired,
transmission-trucked, hitched

to the electronic pulse
of a quick delivery.

We've forgotten, or there's a deeper structure
linguists haven't figured out yet.

If the deaf can sense vibration . . .
If the deaf know a sign as a word . . .

Who's to say silence all these millennia
hasn't been offering its palm?

Dumb as a stone, I think I could begin
a little lip reading. Master the shine-exact English

of the stars. I think I could interpret
the delicate tremble of their light.

Homage to W. S. Graham

Begin with a tendril of ice, white
shadows on snow.
Listen to the footprints of a man's departure,
one who vanished
without even a dream of smoke.

Now the moon rafts down its light
to a lee of willows
and I read again your words:

> *Have I not been trying to use the obstacle*
> *of language well? It freezes round us all.*

To be a spokesman for silence
is hard as hearing
the echo of one's own breath. Yet
if we are to believe in the mouth, the issue

of sound as its own issue,
should we not come to know the manner of
our talk?

> Winter. The still season. Unlike the others, it does not pass over
> but through: a gesture, a finger to the lips to hush.
> Without speech, we have only thought.
> Set down, we bargain for audience,
> we are back to asking for an ear
> anywhere—in the distant hills, in the white fields,
> in the straw, in the husk.

Unless we write to windless space
or rather *for* it . . . there is a difference.

> *Speaking to you and not*
> *knowing if you are there*
> *is not too difficult.*
> *My words are used to that.*

William, why do we keep
testing the deaf air, thinking it can form
a visible line, one that can shore and steady us?

> *A fool's errand . . .*

Yes. And yet—

I believe in the scene
enough to record what I think it has to say:

> These drifts and hollows are ancient runes
> worth every human syllable.
> Listen . . . why do you interrupt?
> Make sure it is deserving.
> In tone. In oath.
> Remember most:

> *Do not expect applause.*

So It Is Written

A story not unlike a story.
A story's grail.

When we happen upon the women
they are looking for a plume,
one that will carry them
through the desert's hoodless hours.

Traveling blinds their eyes.
Soon their hands are wasted,
withered runes.
All they have collected they cannot bear:

the skins of a million purple lizards,
the sun of the sun's white sun.

Time, Mr. Anti-climax
steps out and beats his chest.
And the women? They gather around him,
croon and shuffle their feet,

until dust rises from the shimmering sand,
forms claws full of feathers,
then feathers,
then dust.

ANSWER

A catechism of clouds, sky's white text,
open, unnumbered
                    —the ground's glazed weeds

singing of ice and silence.
Somewhere in between,
heart's chalk-dust swept over the mirror's imaginings.

Well. I didn't mean to write about loneliness,
but here we are; I knock on wood, on glass, on air—
always, there's the quiet crumble of a leaf.

                    No one listening.
What news.
Fall merges into winter.

                    Outside my house, mute trees
peer through the window.
What might they ask, if there were a thing to ask?

How hard it is, to be human.
How hard it is, the flag of our breath
unable to catch the wind.

                    ∿

"If you drew a diamond hand,
five of a kind, in flesh and bone," says altar ego.

Sacrificial poker? For whom? For what?

Mead of glory, I lip your cup,
taste nothing. I come away with a stain,
felt soul mopping up the spill.

We are alone.
We return, our small rooms scattered with offerings.
It is time for a different prayer.

Sky Blood Wind Soliloquy

Whether my thoughts will gather today
or wait for a cold, full moon to fly doesn't matter.

All autumn I wrote nothing, and the wind
ripped up scores of an ancient text with five fierce hands.

Late morning: sun streaks like flying buttresses
fixed to the mountains. Momentary golds.

Nothing in focus but the sky, whose mantra
is a wink. I'm lying low, waiting out my exit.

～

Nineteen degrees, first snow.
Rock cress, white whorls, absent the death kiss.
Johnny-jump-ups still in bloom.
Across the bay, the ridgeline a stretch of terre-verte and violet;
spotlit poplars, Naples yellow, last lieder of the season.

The weather's always a step ahead.
We shouldn't worry about what precedes and follows.
Maybe tomorrow vowels will build to syllables
to strings of sound that scribble the updrafts
like a kited leaf

and by chance now I turn to Paz:

To write poetry
            is learning to read
the hole of writing
            in the writing

and I was so hard at work
looking for the arrangement of words.

~

Poetry, weather, death.
All born of the same alphabet,
all punctuating the same plain.

I stumble alone over
tussock and stone, meaning
poetry is belief.
Another translation would say the same:
outside my window, gibbous moon

hunchback sister, flatheaded muse,
fears the inadequate.
But she still has her business,
spillage of light and a bluntnose course
over ridges and watery hands
that cannot slow her path.
Or so we hope.

~

What sequence
but the sequence of the moon?
Full moon in fall, the old-timers say, first frost.
Not always. When the clouds blow out
our clearest memories are grief
hard as a crescent, soft as a tear.

Here's a theory:
Bloodlet, we build our shrine.
Bloodlet, the wind moves into its dreamtent
and sips the calm.

Rose on the mountainside, rose on the roof
it's traveling, fading, will be gone.

O language, when you are colorless and still,
are you still language?

Elle fait la mort,
she's silent as death:
whispers through a medium of backlit trees.

Arbre à feuille, arbre vert
the deciduous is all abstraction,
the evergreen concrete.

Put something down, said my teacher, Jacob Lawrence.
The night has: palette knife stroke,

lamp-black and manganese violet,
smooth as a requiem, true as breath.

No one is going anywhere this hour.
No one will arrive.

No One Can Separate the Light from the Light

Wild geranium and rose, colors that burnish my heart.
Summer is the month of stealing.
The light will coalesce, grounding its circuit to the noon.
Take this flowered cloth.
Be willing to walk the maze, wearing little, be willing.

A tall wind grazes the lake.
From here all sighs are shallow, although their length is long.
I am reading a woven thing.
Like grass, it bends and breathes.
Like water, it is my closest religion.

A rove: a slightly twisted and extended fiber or sliver.
Like copper, I take my charge.
How wonderful it is to pick up and arc, pick up and arc.
This whole life is debt.
There is no flower that does not buzz, all swollen scent and minute.

Viridescent days.
These hours I wear no halter, for no one will arrive.
Such fine habits.
In these threads of heightened air, I must find my gathering.
Stitch pause to pause.

Terms

Tonight the soul has no argument.
The fireweed are no longer full of fire.
Late August, their petals have all dropped;
white-feather seeds loft
skyward.

I do not care much for passion.
These flowers suit me now—
holding out, their standing
less important than a willingness
to send their terms

to a chimeless, desultory wind.
Even dying it is possible to insist
on a language delicate and quiet,
that maybe will take root
and maybe not.

The Meantime

Only death redeems us,
with its shawl, its quiet wrist,
bearing a music
kind as the slow, sweet ache
of sun on broken clover.

Not that I long for death,
only that part
when we're finally done
wrestling our dew-slicked shadows
on a playing field mown blue-black:

respite from the heavy noise of want,
respite from our tongues, petty as trowels,
from everything difficult to peel off,
envy and deceit, formfitting
as a pair of wet rubber gloves.

Death is our cause.
It makes us better, to think of it.
But sometimes, in the dusk
or in the thin, rose light of morning

we wake. There is a hand
at the gate of our shut hearts, waiting
for guidance:

a voice mild as a southern wind
whispering, *just one moment,*
lift, unlatch.

Away from the Day Shift's Bullhorn and Dazzle

At night, alone in our own rooms, we lie
quietly, no other to watch us listen
as the dark talks solemnly to the moon
or the wind steps lightly outside the window.

This is speech at its best,
the landscape's proper grammar,
a gray animal in the distance
pitching its muted clarinet to the sky's roof.

How did Li Ch'ing-chao, "most famous and accomplished
of Chinese women poets," put it?
Last night, among the deep snows of the village,
One blossom opened.

Grace of the singular, polar star,
anoint the quick and the coarse-throated.
Give us a measure's hush, soft-light our mouths,
allow us your gentle wash.

CREDO

~

Because the leaves fall softly when they drop,
I will follow the vole's track.

~

Because my blood is the shape of sky,
I will look not to man or woman.

~

A theory of beauty? Listen:
wing and toil, breath.

~

All measure is a great swing
suspended by the finest thread of air.

~

Assonance delivers soul,
consonance its quickened echo.

~

In moonlight
even the stopped bell rings.

~

There is economy that is cold,
cold that is the heart's great gladness.

Vestiges

Already the light shepherds its spirit
to the west; already the clouds darken
to a kinder definition. I am better now,
though my earlier rue is not lost.
It has only moved on into distant hills
brushed with indigo, snow, and spruce;
it has only stepped, like a small,
four-legged brute into the crèche of night
and bedded down, reserving its final, lonely right
to remain silent.

The world at such times is a furl of affirmation.
Soon I will turn to go back inside,
cross this bay of windswept ice,
not even a star to guide me.
And to those who've led me to believe
in a trail of assurances they were unable to deliver,
I give my thanks. I'll chance it home
cleansed of the nascent smell of incense.
Summer will arrive. I'll make a jacket
of silverweed and wool.
I will not kill the animal.

April Psalm

Furnish this body
as you would the tree,
lending the hidden root a wick

and the skin
a silver flame;
leave

my shadow warm
as, fixed to earth,
I turn and straighten to your pull.

It was winter's snow
that leaned me down,
now

I stretch—I ask
O spring
that your lift be steady and easy.

Know that I know
it is our work,
my limbs willing

to break from this curb
of sullen ice,
the slowly melting crust.

Unpublished

Clouds five thousand, scattered,
sun-clumps like Golden *Pholiota*
in the early evening sky.
The lake is still.

Two eagles have let down
somewhere in a hush of spruce,
even the memory of their wings declining.
Here all reference stalls

as light scripts its own unbodied book:
clean angle and swirl on vellum slope
—a guilded, ancient lettering—
that lengthens, climbs, descends . . .

But I stop, wanting for once
nothing adorned to describe the dusk
that covers our every imprint now
with perfect, though equally perishable, shadows.

The Art of Being

The fern in the rain breathes the silver message.
Stay, lie low. Play your dark reeds
and relearn the beauty of absorption.
There is nothing beyond the rotten log
covered with leaves and needles.
Forget the light emerging with its golden wick.
Raise your face to the water-laden frond.
A thousand blossoms will fall into your arms.

SEVEN COUPLETS TO AWAKENING

Dusk: a small shelf beyond a wall
trying to support the day's great body.

Smoother and smoother the wind,
seamless as the lining of a quiet thought.

Listen closely: all through the heart's arteries a red-backed vole
scurries for a last tidbit of time.

Behind the solemn eyelid of the night
stars are extending their roots.

Now is the time to touch the cooling furnaces,
to let the skin measure its distance outside the earth.

Frail suspension between a bell of light
and the timbre of a thinning star.

Rush nothing. Wakening is a vine
climbing out from the moon's last glimmer.

Grass Studies

If we can't be aether,
I thought we might settle for grass,
and why not *slender wheat*, which serves
as forage for wildlife? Less populous

than *bluejoint*, it wasn't grown in Europe
like *canary*—as seed for captive songbirds—
or used the way the Chippewa used *foxtail*—
to kill their troublesome dogs.
(A knife to the throat is considerably swifter.)

But who among us can know her purpose?
It's just the sound of *slender wheat*
I like, although *oat grass* isn't bad,
or *timothy*, or *northern brome*,
not to be confused with another variety that's *smooth*
and habitat-invasive.

It's hard to know what's natural,
hard to learn that the grain of *slender wheat*
is sometimes infected with ergot,
a fungus causing lameness or necrosis.

Still, the field is beautiful—
there are grasses taller than my head.
I'm drawn to the delicacy of inflorescence,
the bend of the awn in wind.

Hold in the Hand Your Many Vows

What better morning to profess belief
than this; what better hour to hear

settling on the grate the burning wood,
how easy to purge the conditional.

Here, one can wake to a range of mountains
graphing the same end leaf of sky

and think *this is the place*
to white-out revelation's burden.

What's coming? Who cares? No spirit ever knocked
but entered and swept clean the mind.

Take what you have, be kind, and rest.
The poplars stand golden and tall.

Each word, behold, is a seed of light.
Each line we lift to our own horizon.

～

Loving is half of believing, wrote Victor Hugo.
I'd say the other half is pruning hope.

Isn't that what the world does, arriving
with its shears of storm and ash

while leaves pinwheel and glint
in the lush, the infinite now?

Sure, our handiwork yellows and curls,
sure the mirror is filmed with dust

but still the syllable holds out
proofing our music for a false step,

gracing the shadow of the purposed brow.
"When you have found the Buddha, slay him."

The secret's not to look. Watch how the wind keeps to its task,
loosens and rocks the tree, no heed for the thought of dying.

Sterna paradisaea

I love the tern, when it sweeps, china-white
against the ridge of variegated green,
its way of flashing through

once in a random evening, glide
more elegant than a gull's, tail an open shears
arrested just before the act of cutting.

And when the bird is gone,
we cannot stay forever watching
the rose-gray light and the lake, whose color

—mountain-blue in early summer—
is turquoise-emerald by July, as silt
moves down from the upper glaciers.

We're coming close when a thing that's passed
becomes a sheen for which we cease to yearn,
and we're ready to welcome night's granite cast.

Layaway

I'll take this light
cardigan,
woven
of sunset amber and rose;

wrapped
in tissue it should keep clean
until my return

until these shell-
white bones become
a sprinkling of purer dust.

STRAND

Invisible, before our angle's right
or the sun comes out of shadow.
What's threaded glints eternal,
even at night in sallow rooms
where we toil for hours in a straight-backed chair
at a cluttered desk, fingering the abacus,
counting up loneliness and despair.
There's always more.
Meanwhile, if we're lucky, the wolf spider will detach
from the corner window, begin its long descent
by way of silk and slow motion
and we'll remember to touch one bead
that has all the properties of dew,
to move it back and forth
until zero is the sum of merit,
until our hand is wind
and the wooden rod is nudged to a bend and sway.

A Hand Half in Darkness

The year always begins for me in September
when loss is fully apparent,
deliquescent light sliding back
into its house of bone.
Winter retreat coming on.
But also a coming to, relearning

the edges of things:
water dipper's curve, open mouth
of cup as we drink our tea
and trace the smooth ceramic circle.

Touch is what we lose in summer
when we are all sight, hunters
of color; we know the rose but not
the imperceptible weight of petals.

So I long for fall, our time
to bring in the birch, to lift
the dense and wind-dried wood,
return to a layering of fine paper.

Now the sky delivers its black ink.
Now our candles mirror the stars,
a wax and cling to the soul's wick.
O shape within, O reach, O incantation.

Notes

"Weights, Measures." The italicized lines in stanza four are from *Omensetter's Luck* by William Gass.

"Statue Freestanding." *Contrapposto* is Italian for "set against." It was a method developed by the Greeks to represent freedom of movement in a figure.

"Painting, Beginning." *Grisaille* is a style of monochromatic painting in shades of gray.

"No One Can Separate the Light from the Light." The title is taken from the poem "A Journal of True Confessions" by Charles Wright.

"Away from the Day Shift's Bullhorn and Dazzle." The quote is by Robert Payne, editor of *The White Pony: An Anthology of Chinese Poetry* (1960), which includes Li-Ch'ing-chao's poem "Spring Returns." The two lines in italics are excerpted from this piece.

"A Hand Half in Darkness." The title is taken from the poem "A Winter Light" by John Haines.

"*Sterna paradisaea.*" Latin name for the arctic tern.

"Hold in the Hand Your Many Vows." Eastern adage: "When you have found the Buddha, slay him."

Biographical Note

Anne Coray's poetry collections include *Bone Strings* and *Violet Transparent*. She is coauthor of *Lake Clark National Park and Preserve* and coeditor of *Crosscurrents North: Alaskans on the Environment*. Twice nominated for the Pushcart and the recipient of grants and a fellowship from the Alaska State Council on the Arts and an Individual Artist Project Award from the Rasmuson Foundation, she lives at her birthplace on remote Qizhjeh Vena (Lake Clark) in southwest Alaska.